THE GREAT BIBLE DISCOVERY

THE GOOD NEWS

THE BIBLE IS A BEST-SELLER. IT IS ALSO ONE OF THE MASTER-WORKS OF WORLD LITERATURE - SO IMPORTANT THAT UNIVERSITIES TODAY TEACH 'NON-RELIGIOUS' BIBLE COURSES TO HELP STUDENTS WHO CHOOSE TO STUDY WESTERN LITERATURE.

THE BIBLE POSSESSES AN AMAZING POWER TO FASCINATE YOUNG AND OLD ALIKE.

ONE REASON FOR THIS UNIVERSAL APPEAL IS THAT IT DEALS WITH BASIC HUMAN LONGINGS, EMOTIONS, RELATIONSHIPS. 'ALL THE WORLD IS HERE.' ANOTHER REASON IS THAT SO MUCH OF THE BIBLE CONSISTS OF STORIES. THEY ARE FULL OF MEANING BUT EASY TO REMEMBER.

HERE ARE THOSE STORIES, PRESENTED SIMPLY AND WITH A MINIMUM OF EXPLANATION. WE HAVE LEFT THE TEXT TO SPEAK FOR ITSELF. GIFTED ARTISTS USE THE ACTION-STRIP TECHNIQUE TO BRING THE BIBLE'S DEEP MESSAGE TO READERS OF ALL AGES. THEIR DRAWINGS ARE BASED ON INFORMATION FROM ARCHAEOLOGICAL DISCOVERIES COVERING FIFTEEN CENTURIES.

AN ANCIENT BOOK - PRESENTED FOR THE PEOPLE OF THE SECOND MILLENNIUM. A RELIGIOUS BOOK - PRESENTED FREE FROM THE INTERPRETATION OF ANY PARTICULAR CHURCH. A UNIVERSAL BOOK - PRESENTED IN A FORM THAT ALL MAY ENJOY.

M
publishing
CARLISLE, UK

19

THE GOOD NEWS

The four books from which we learn most about the life of Jesus are called 'gospels'. The word 'gospel' means 'good news'. But what was the good news contained in the gospels? In a word, salvation. Throughout their history the Hebrews had come to realise that God is the true king of the world and that he planned to destroy the power of evil and to deliver his people. In Old Testament times he had sent 'saviours' such as Moses and David. But Israel looked forward to a New Age when God's mighty power as their saving King would be fully seen. The good news of the gospels is that in Jesus this 'King-dom (or kingship) of God' had appeared to save all humankind..

Jesus' power over disease and demonic forces showed God's saving power in a dramatic way. Although he taught his disciples to pray 'Your kingdom come', he also insisted that it was already active in the world.

The gospels are not straightforward 'biographies' of Jesus as we understand that word today. They supply four different portraits of the Man who expressed God's saving power in action. Even during the life of Jesus, and then following his death and resurrection, his teaching will have been memorized and written down. His followers will have recalled his wonderful deeds. The apostles will have told the stories of such great events as the Passion and Resurrection. Four writers, themselves apostles, or friends of the apostles, selected from this rich store of sayings and deeds, preserving what was both true and useful for evangelism and Christian teaching and worship.

According to a very old tradition the author of Mark was Peter's interpreter and he based his gospel on Peter's memories. It would have been especially encouraging for Christians at Rome, who suffered fierce persecution in AD 65.

The gospel bearing the name of Matthew seems to have been compiled for the use of Christian Jews. It stresses the way Jesus fulfilled the Old Testament law and messianic prophecies. It arranges the teaching of Jesus in a way that would make it easier to memorize.

Luke was a friend and colleague of Paul. In his travels he was able to meet eyewitnesses of the events of Jesus' life. His gospel was intended to appeal to non-Jews who were interested in the origins and nature of Christianity.

John's gospel shows Jesus' eternal significance. Sometimes John paraphrases things he had heard Jesus say, in order to bring out their inner meaning. For him the miracles were 'signs' of what it means to experience salvation.

The gospel writers were not chiefly concerned to satisfy historical curiosity. The purpose of the gospels is to help people believe in Jesus and follow him more closely.

First published as *Découvrir la Bible* 1983

First edition © Librairie Larousse 1983
English translation © Daan Retief Publishers 1990
24-volume series adaptation by Mike Jacklin © Knowledge Unlimited 1994
This edition © OM Publishing 1995

01 00 99 98 97 96 95   7 6 5 4 3 2 1

OM Publishing is an imprint of Send the Light Ltd.,
P.O. Box 300, Carlisle, Cumbria CA3 0QS, U.K.

Series editor: D. Roy Briggs
English translation: Bethan Uden
Introductions: Peter Cousins

British Library Cataloguing in Publication Data
A catalogue record for this book is available from the British Library
ISBN 1-85078-223-7

Printed in Singapore by Tien Wah Press (Pte) Ltd.

MATTHEW 1-8   MARK 1-3
LUKE 1-8   JOHN 1-2

JOHN THE BAPTIST AND JESUS

IN THE TIME OF KING HEROD THERE WAS IN JERUSALEM A TEMPLE PRIEST CALLED **ZACHARIAH**. HE WAS ALWAYS BEGGING GOD TO BLESS HIM AND HIS WIFE WITH A CHILD, EVEN THOUGH THEY WERE BOTH OLD.

SCENARIO: Etienne DAHLER
DRAWING: Paolo ELEUTERI-SERPIERI

ZACHARIAH, THE LOT'S FALLEN TO YOU TO BURN THE INCENSE IN THE HOUSE OF THE LORD.

BLESSED BE THE HOLY ONE OF ISRAEL!

ZACHARIAH WENT INTO THE TEMPLE TO CARRY OUT HIS PRIESTLY DUTIES.

HE'S A LONG TIME ... WHAT'S GOING ON?

AS LONG AS HE'S NOT BEEN OVER-WHELMED BY THE LORD'S PRESENCE! IT'S HAPPENED TO OTHER PEOPLE...

HERE HE COMES!

HE'S DUMB! HE CAN'T SAY ANYTHING!

HE MUST HAVE HAD A VISION!

WHEN ZACHARIAH HAD COMPLETED HIS DUTY AT THE TEMPLE, HE WENT BACK TO HIS VILLAGE CLOSE TO JERUSALEM.

MEANWHILE IN NAZARETH, A GALILEAN VILLAGE SOME 160 KILOMETRES NORTH OF JERUSALEM...

LET'S GO BACK NOW, MARY. THE SUN'S SETTING...

MY BASKET'S FULL TOO.

OH, MARY, YOUR FIANCÉ JOSEPH WAS HERE. HE'LL COME BACK LATER.

MARY WENT HOME AND FOUND HER MOTHER ANNE IN THE DOORWAY WAITING FOR HER...

A FEW MONTHS LATER...

ZACHARIAH, THE LORD'S ANSWERED OUR PRAYER. I'M EXPECTING A CHILD.

WAIT FOR ME! I'M COMING!

THAT EVENING...

TODAY WE DREW UP OUR MARRIAGE CONTRACT WITH THE RABBI.

THAT'S GOOD! I'M HAPPY TO HAVE A DESCENDANT OF DAVID AS A SON-IN-LAW!

A FEW DAYS LATER...

AFTER A JOURNEY OF SEVERAL DAYS...

ZACHARIAH! ELIZABETH! YOUR COUSIN MARY IS HERE!

PEACE BE WITH YOU, ELIZABETH!

...AND WITH YOU, MARY.

YOU ARE THE MOST BLESSED OF ALL WOMEN AND BLESSED IS THE CHILD YOU WILL BEAR.

BUT HOW DO YOU KNOW, ELIZABETH?

AND YOU, MARY? NOBODY ELSE KNOWS THAT I'M EXPECTING A CHILD!

THE LORD'S GREAT! I DANCE WITH JOY FOR MY GOD WHO HAS SAVED ME!

MARY...
IT'S IMPOSSIBLE...
MARY...

JOSEPH WENT TO GET ADVICE FROM THE RABBI.

IT'S VERY SIMPLE, JOSEPH. IF THE CHILD'S YOURS, THE TORAH DOESN'T CONDEMN YOU. YOU ARE, IN FACT, MARRIED. BUT IF THE CHILD ISN'T YOURS, YOU MUST CANCEL THE CONTRACT WITH MARY, AND...

AND?

...SHE'LL BE STONED... THAT'S THE LAW.

THAT SAME NIGHT JOSEPH WAS DEEPLY DISTURBED, WHEN...

JOSEPH, DON'T BE AFRAID TO TAKE MARY AS YOUR WIFE. THE CHILD SHE CARRIES IS THE FRUIT OF THE HOLY SPIRIT.

IT WILL BE A BOY. YOU'LL CALL HIM JESUS.*

* God saves.

10

LITTLE EPHRAIM CAME BACK WITH ONE OF HIS SISTERS...

HAS THE BABY COME ALREADY?

YES, IT'S A BOY!

I'LL SEE TO MARY. PUT THE CHILD IN THE MANGER; THE DONKEY'S BREATH WILL KEEP HIM WARM.

CAN WE COME IN?

IT IS NOT THE BEST TIME!

WE'VE COME TO SEE THE LITTLE ONE!

LATER THAT SAME NIGHT SOME SHEPHERDS ARRIVED.

* Men who studied the stars.

EIGHT DAYS LATER THE CHILD WAS CIRCUMCISED AND GIVEN THE NAME JESUS. FAR AWAY, SOMEWHERE IN ARABIA, MAGI*...

IT'S EXACTLY LIKE THE ANGEL SAID!

TODAY YOUR SAVIOUR'S BEEN BORN!

THERE IT IS! A NEW STAR'S JUST APPEARED!

WE'VE WORKED IT OUT! IT'S THE MESSIAH'S STAR!

19

THE SAME NIGHT THEY GATHERED FOR THE PASSOVER MEAL.

BLESSED BE THE LORD OUR GOD, KING OF THE UNIVERSE, WHO DELIVERED OUR ANCESTORS FROM EGYPT, AND HAS ENABLED US TO REACH THIS NIGHT AND TO EAT THE PASSOVER BREAD.

SOON IT WAS TIME TO SET OUT BACK TO NAZARETH.

JESUS? HE MUST BE WITH THE YOUNGSTERS AT THE BACK.

NO, I'VE BEEN THERE. NO ONE'S SEEN HIM...

THEY ASKED EVERYWHERE, BUT NO ONE COULD HELP THEM.

YOU MUST GO BACK TO JERUSALEM.

IN THE END, AFTER SEARCHING FOR THREE DAYS...

WHERE DO YOU COME FROM, MY BOY, AND WHERE DID YOU LEARN ALL THESE THINGS?

HE KNOWS THE SCRIPTURES PERFECTLY, AND HAS AN ANSWER TO EVERY QUESTION!

THERE HE IS!

MY CHILD, YOU HAD US SO WORRIED!

WHY DID YOU HUNT FOR ME? DIDN'T YOU KNOW I WOULD BE IN MY FATHER'S HOUSE?

YOUR SON'S AMAZED US WITH HIS WISDOM! WATCH OVER HIM CAREFULLY!

23

JESUS in Galilee

SCENARIO: Etienne DAHLER
DRAWING: Paolo ELEUTERI-SERPIERI

THEN THE SPIRIT SENT JESUS INTO THE DESERT. HE WAS TEMPTED BY SATAN FOR 40 DAYS.

BE GONE, SATAN! FOR IT IS WRITTEN: YOU SHALL NOT TEMPT THE LORD YOUR GOD!

THEN JESUS WENT BACK TO THE JORDAN VALLEY.

IT IS HE, ANDREW; I'M SURE. THE BAPTIST POINTED HIM OUT TO US!

WELL, COME ON THEN!

WE'RE BOTH DISCIPLES OF JOHN THE BAPTIST, AND...

RABBI, WHERE ARE YOU STAYING?

COME AND SEE.

TOMORROW I MUST GO AND TELL MY BROTHER SIMON ABOUT YOU.

WHILE ANDREW SET OFF FOR LAKE TIBERIAS, TWO MEN CAME TO JOHN THE BAPTIST ON THE BANKS OF THE JORDAN.

JOHN! HEROD'S GUARDS ARE COMING TO ARREST YOU!

QUICKLY! YOU STILL HAVE TIME TO ESCAPE!

NO, THE TIME HAS COME.

ARREST HIM!

HE MUST BECOME GREATER, WHILE I BECOME LESS.

THE NEXT DAY, SIMON...

MOVE BACK! LET HIM THROUGH!

YOU, FOLLOW ME!

IT'S PHILIP, MASTER! HE LIVES NEARBY.

MASTER, LET ME GO ON AHEAD...

NATHANAEL! NATHANAEL!

NATHANAEL, WE'VE FOUND THE ONE THE LAW AND THE PROPHETS SPEAK OF: IT'S JESUS OF NAZARETH!

CAN ANYTHING GOOD COME OUT OF NAZARETH, PHILIP?

COME AND SEE FOR YOURSELF, NATHANAEL!

MARY SPOKE TO HIM
DURING THE MEAL...

THEY'VE RUN OUT OF WINE...

WHAT DO YOU WANT ME TO DO? MY TIME'S NOT YET COME...

DO EVERYTHING HE TELLS YOU TO!

FILL THESE JARS WITH WATER!

TAKE SOME TO THE MASTER OF CEREMONIES.

WHAT A SURPRISE! THE BRIDEGROOM'S KEPT HIS BEST WINE TO THE END.

THIS WORD OF SCRIPTURE HAS COME TRUE TODAY!

WHAT ARE YOU SAYING? ONLY THE MESSIAH CAN FULFIL THAT PROPHECY!

AREN'T YOU JOSEPH'S SON? WHO DO YOU THINK YOU ARE?

IT'S TRUE THAT NO PROPHET'S TREATED WELL IN HIS OWN LAND.

THEY CHASED HIM OUT OF THE TOWN AND DRAGGED HIM TO THE EDGE OF A CLIFF TO THROW HIM OVER.

SILENCE HIM!

OUT WITH THE IMPOSTOR!

SEIZE HIM WHEN HE COMES OUT!

DON'T DO SUCH A SINFUL THING!

THEN THEY LET HIM GO.

THE NEXT MORNING, AFTER HE'D PRAYED FOR A LONG TIME ...

WE MUST MOVE ON! OTHER TOWNS MUST ALSO HEAR ABOUT THE KINGDOM OF GOD.

JESUS PREACHED IN THE SYNAGOGUES ALL OVER GALILEE, HEALING THE SICK AND DRIVING OUT EVIL SPIRITS.

ALL THOSE PEOPLE AROUND HIM! IT WORRIES ME...

I WONDER WHAT JERUSALEM'S GOING TO THINK.

ALONG THE ROAD...

JESUS! IT'S A LEPER! KEEP BACK!

COME BACK! HE'S UNCLEAN!

YOU CAN MAKE ME CLEAN, IF YOU WANT TO.

I WILL! BE HEALED!

GO, SHOW YOURSELF TO THE PRIEST, AND MAKE THE OFFERING FOR YOUR HEALING, AS MOSES LAID DOWN.

37

THE NEXT SABBATH JESUS WAS TEACHING IN THE SYNAGOGUE. THERE WAS A MAN WHOSE RIGHT HAND WAS PARALYSED.

STAND UP, AND COME HERE!

IF HE DARES TO HEAL HIM, WE'LL BE ABLE TO ACCUSE HIM.

I ASK YOU: WHICH IS RIGHT – TO DO EVIL ON THE SABBATH, OR TO DO GOOD?

GOOD! THEN STRETCH OUT YOUR HAND!

THE PHARISEES KEPT QUIET...

HE'S HEALED!

ALLELUIA!

GOD IS ALL-POWERFUL!

NOW WE KNOW ENOUGH.

HE CLAIMS TO BE LORD OF THE SABBATH, AND BEHAVES LIKE IT TOO!

THAT'S BLASPHEMY! GOD ALONE IS LORD OF THE SABBATH!

WORST OF ALL, HE ATTRACTS CROWDS. EVERY DAY MORE PEOPLE FOLLOW HIM.

WE MUST ACT QUICKLY, BEFORE THEY BECOME TOO POWERFUL.

JESUS SPENT THE NEXT NIGHT ON THE MOUNTAIN, PRAYING.

WHEN DAYLIGHT CAME, HE BROUGHT HIS DISCIPLES TOGETHER AND CHOSE 12 OF THEM. HE CALLED THEM APOSTLES.

PETER AND ANDREW, JAMES AND JOHN, PHILIP AND BARTHOLOMEW, MATTHEW, THOMAS, JAMES...

...SIMON, JUDE, AND JUDAS...

THE ISCARIOT? BUT HE'S NOT EVEN A GALILEAN!

THAT'S WHAT I SAID: JUDAS ISCARIOT!

SOME TIME LATER, A PHARISEE CAME TO SEE JESUS.

MY NAME'S SIMON. I LIVE NEARBY. WILL YOU COME AND EAT AT MY TABLE?

OF COURSE, SIMON! I NEVER REFUSE TO GO WHERE I'M INVITED.

THAT EVENING, DURING THE MEAL...

WOMAN, WHAT ARE YOU DOING HERE? IN THE HOUSE OF A GOOD MAN?

I DON'T UNDERSTAND. YOU SAY THAT YOU FULFIL THE LAW, BUT YOU SEEM TO SCORN IT...

IF HE WERE A PROPHET, HE'D KNOW WHAT SORT OF WOMAN WAS TOUCHING HIM!